A Practical Approach to

Selecting, Training, and Using Draft Horses

by
Merle E. Saxon

Heart Prairie Press
Whitewater, Wisconsin

A hard-cover edition was first published in 1976 by The Pawnee Republican, Pawnee, Nebraska.

This soft-cover edition was published in 1993 by:
Heart Prairie Press
P. O. Box 332
Whitewater, Wisconsin 53190
USA

Produced in its entirety in the United States of America.

Publisher's Cataloging in Publication Data
Sason, Merle E., 1909-1991
    A practical approach to selecting, training, and using draft horses / by Merle E. Saxon. -- [Rev. ed.]
    p. cm.
    Rev. ed of work first published in 1976, including a new autobiographical section.
    ISBN 1-882199-01-4
    1. Draft horses. 2. Sason, Merle E., 1909-1991. 3. Farmers--Nebraska--Biography.   I. Title.
SF311.S39 1993   636.1'5
                                            QB193-1277

Introduction

There is a growing interest in draft horses by younger folk. It seems many professional people, business people, school teachers, and people from all walks of life have become interested in owning draft horses — some as a hobby, some for relaxation from daily routines, others as a way of advertising, in an attractive manner, many types of business. There is also the pride of ownership, and the challenge that exists between man and beast as to who is in control.

For a newcomer in the draft horse world there is a lot to learn in a relatively short time. Lack of knowledge and experience can be costly and ruinous to equipment, animals, and man. This book has been produced in the hope it will be useful as a guide and as a caution to inexperienced horsemen.

The draft horse industry welcomes and appreciates this interest in draft horses by younger people, and we hope to encourage and assist in making them horsemen through the advice and methods set forth in this book.

The suggestions and ideas set forth in this book were arrived at through a lifetime of association with draft animals. My father was a horseman, and I have been exposed to horses and mules my entire life. I am now at the rocking chair age, and am still raising Belgians. I break my own colts and custom break quite a few each year.

Every horseman has his own way of handling colts and horses. The methods and ideas that follow in this book will not be accepted by all as the proper way, but they have worked well for me.

Acknowledgments

I hereby wish to express my thanks and appreciation to those who have helped with the production of this book. To W. H. Thompson of Pawnee City, Nebraska, for his help in printing this material. To Miss Nancy Foulks for typing the manuscript. To Philip Foster and Marvin Chappalear for camera work. And also to my wife, Rachel, for her help and encouragement with this project.

Contents

Careful Selection Very Important

Selection is very important in draft horses, especially so today, since they are not called upon to do the work they used to do, day after day. When they were the chief source of power on the farms and for transportation most any stubborn old hammerhead could be worn down into submission but now that they are used more or less for show or as a hobby such as parades and the like, disposition or temperament is very important.

A kind, gentle nature in a horse is bred in, or is a hereditary trait, as a general rule. Of course there are exceptions to all rules.

Disposition can be determined to quite a large degree by studying the subject's head. Of course this would not hold true if a horse has been mistreated or spoiled in some manner, with poor judgement on the part of the handler. Any horse can be spoiled regardless of the heredity or disposition by being mishandled or misused by careless or inexperienced handlers.

The profile of a horse's face usually is a pretty accurate indication of his nature or temperament. A curved or Roman nose might well indicate stubbornness or strong will. A dished face quite often signifies a sulky, even treacherous nature. The eyes should be large and open. Heavy brows and deep wrinkles over the eyes indicate a nervous, suspi-

The author with a pair of his favorites. These mares produce a fine pair of colts each year, besides doing the chores and parade duty.

7

cious temperament. The ears should be set quite wide apart and be the right size and shape for the breed concerned. A long, sharp pointed ear indicates a nervous, ill-tempered animal. The expression "its ears came out of the same hole" indicates a horse with limited brain capacity and lacking in intelligence and ability. These close-set ears are also a very good indication of a balky horse, lacking in courage and not very apt to cooperate with the driver.

Other points to consider when selecting a draft horse are its conformation of body. The length of the body is quite important. Too long a back and body indicate a hard keeper, often referred to as a "corn crib". Too much length of body does not give a balanced appearance to an animal. Too short a body is not desirable either. The length of the body should be average or normal for the particular breed.

The neck should be of good length, and set well up, as a low-headed horse never looks good. The throat should be clean and not too thick. This indicates good wind, where a short heavy-necked horse often lacks this quality. The

A team showing good length of body and neck — the kind that produce good, straight colts because they have room to carry them.

circumference of the heart girth should be quite large. This gives lung capacity which is necessary and important.

The legs and feet are other points to scrutinize carefully. The legs should be set well under the horse. Common faults of the front legs are "calf legged" in which the legs drop back at the knees. This is a weakness and it can become worse under heavy strain. "Buck knees" is another defect of the front legs where the lower leg extends forward, also an objectionable trait.

The feet should be set straight with the horse's body. Feet that turn in are known as "pigeon toed" and those that turn out as "coon footed". Neither is good and they lessen the value of the animal as well as affecting its gait and appearance. The hind or back legs of a draft horse are very important as this is the power end of the animal. The hock or middle joint of the back leg should be smooth and quite flat, not too thick or meaty. The hock should have just enough set so a pole stood behind the horse will stand straight up and down, touching the butt, the cap of the hock, and the fetlock.

The foot of the horse is one of his most necessary and important assets. It has been wisely said, "no foot, no horse". The type of foot varies somewhat in different draft breeds, but all should be of good, tough texture, with a wide heel and the size of the foot in proportion to the size and weight of the animal. A horse with correct feet will bear his weight evenly on his feet. Some are inclined to walk heavy on one side of the foot. This is quite objectionable as the appearance and gait of the horse are adversely affected and the gradual effect on its feet and legs is bad, causing side bones and other problems with bones and tendons.

Color, markings, and general conformation should be in keeping with the particular breed concerned. For example, sorrel is the predominant color in Belgian horses in America. Black and grey are the most common color for Percherons. Black, all shades of brown and bay, and roan, with lots of white trimming on the legs and the bald face are the most common Clydesdale colors. The Suffolk breed runs pretty true in color with most of them a chestnut sorrel with very little markings of the face or legs.

It is strictly a matter of choice or opinion which breed of draft horse one should have, but it is something that should be considered very carefully before buying. If you are buying foundation breeding stock you must be very cautious as physical characteristics and temperaments (disposition) are handed down through generations. It is definitely important to start with the right kind.

Draft horses are most often worked or driven in pairs. It is therefore necessary that a team or pair of horses have quite the same temperament, and be gaited alike. It is not very pleasurable to drive a pair when one horse is willing to do it all, and the other is willing that he should. This aspect of matching a team is much more important than matching for appearance, but the latter is also important. There is a lot of satisfaction and pride in having a well-matched team that drive well together. General conformation, coloring, and markings should all be considered when matching a team. A pair with similar blood lines are more apt to mate in the qualities mentioned

What Kind of Horse for Beginners? Who is a Horseman?

A person not familiar with driving draft horses should surely begin with a gentle, well-broke team that has been in good hands, and which has a good disposition. They should be of mature age, 7 or over. Young, immature horses are easily spoiled by an experienced driver, even if they are considered broke and handle quite well.

Breaking a horse to drive and work amounts to simply teaching him the proper habits. This takes time and patience on the part of the trainer. The breaking or training is to teach the horse to cooperate with its master in the various ways in which it is asked to perform, and to prevent the development of bad habits.

A person should have a love of horses if one considers owning a team of horses. It is often stated that this is an inherited trait, and that either you have the desire and ability to work with horses or you don't.

The horse is quite an intelligent animal, and can easily sum up a person's attitude. The driver's tensions and fears are quite readily detected by a horse, and greatly affect his temperament. This confirms the fact that a nervous, quarrelsome person is not too apt to get along well with horses.

Starting the Young Horse in Harness

A young, unbroke horse should first be taught discipline. He should be taught to respect you and to obey your commands. Horses vary greatly in their learning capacity, and in their willingness to cooperate with a trainer. It is quite necessary to get the horse to have confidence in his master. When this is accomplished they become much more relaxed and cooperative, and become less fearful of the many new problems they must face.

If a colt has never been handled and is not halter-broke he has much to learn in a short period of time. We will assume the colt is broke to tie and he understands that man is not his worst enemy, but that he has had very little handling to gentle him.

I like to break a colt to the side line, regardless of how gentle he is. This means taking a hind foot off the ground with a soft rope secured around the horse's neck. This renders him pretty much helpless, as he can't kick or strike, but instead pretty well has to keep the other three feet on the ground. They will usually fight this the first time, but soon they become accustomed to it. This makes working around the colt much safer and they learn to stand still to be curried and harnessed.

If a colt is jumpy and touchy about everything that happens around him the side line should be put on and he should be sacked out until he loses this fear of everything that moves or touches him. Some horses can be pretty bad about this, but it has to be pretty well overcome before he can proceed much further with his training. He is going to run into a lot of things that will spook him if he maintains a jumpy, belligerent attitude.

Patience on the part of the trainer is a must as a colt is going to do a lot of wrong things before he gets in the habit of doing them right. As has been stated before, breaking a horse is merely teaching him habits of what you want him to do, and discouraging bad habits he might acquire.

A whip is a necessity, but must be used with discernment. A whip used wisely will help the colt to see things your way easier. It should be applied as punishment for disobedience or stubbornness, and to encourage him to do the trainer's will. Never, never should the trainer lose his cool and "knock the hell out of a colt" so to speak. The horse has won the argument if this happens, and a lot of previous training has been undone.

The side-line is a quick, effective way to get control of a colt that refuses to cooperate.

More Advanced Training

After a young horse is familiar with the harness and bridle, and especially with the bit, he is ready to perform some simple duties. It is best not to push him too fast — just let him get the hang of what he is doing. Talk to him and encourage him when he does things well. Do not pressure him too hard or he will get excited and become disobedient. Always be firm in what you want done and never let the horse make the decisions. Finally, don't get angry if all doesn't go as expected.

For the first lesson I like to harness and bridle the colt and circle him on a long line. Circle him in both directions until he performs this task quite willingly. When this is accomplished he will have had a good lesson in obedience, will be used to the feel and rattle of the harness, and will have some experience with the bit. He will have begun to respond to the trainer's will and overcome some of his doubts and fears. It is quite necessary to have a whip in hand to accomplish this lesson at first but it should be used lightly and not abusively, unless the horse will absolutely not cooperate.

During this long line session he should be given his preliminary training in the meaning of "Whoa". On the command, "Whoa", he should be stopped gently at first and more abruptly as the lesson proceeds. Most horses soon learn to respond to this command, especially if they are getting a little weary. Also, the starting command should be taught at this period of training, giving a light tap with the whip at first to cue the colt. This too is generally easily taught to the beginner. There is a great difference in horses as to how quickly they respond to commands of the trainer. Some are more alert than others, some cooperate more readily, and some just stubbornly resist the trainer's will. As a result the time needed for this training varies greatly.

For this part of the training I tie the rope (long line) to the halter and run it through the bit ring, preferably a large, straight bit known as a "log bit".

I like to drive a colt single for his first few drives, using a strong, light rope for lines, working him in a small yard, or better yet, in an inside arena if one is available. This way they can be taught to steer and stop and start. They also learn to stand and become more bit-wise. All this advance training makes them much more at ease when they are hitched to a vehicle with another horse.

Circling to the left on the long line. When this feat is performed well a colt has learned a lot about doing the trainer's will.

Starting the reverse on the long line.

They should be circled both right and left as they have to be developed on both sides.

Time for that First Hitch

By far the best way to hitch a colt for the first few hitches is to hitch him with a well-broke, gentle horse, tying the colt with his halter to the broke horse's hame ring. I like to run a light rope around the rear end of both horses, running it through the lead-up straps of the breeching to suspend it. Tie this rope to the outside breast-strap ring of the hames of each horse, giving enough slack so they can spread a couple of feet apart. This teaches the colt to drive straight ahead, and keeps them from swinging out to see what is going on behind them. It also gives the broke horse a chance to pretty well control the colt. It is good training to drive them hitched together in this manner for a while before they are

Showing a rope around the rear end of the team. This keeps colts in line, and prevents them from spreading or turning inside or out.

hitched to any vehicle. The colt get accustomed to walking alongside the other horse and is pretty well obliged to stop and start on command. They should also be taught to turn either way, turning first to the broke horse and then gradually taught to turn to the colt.

It is good also to let them stand for a while. The colt generally will be fretful at first, but if the broke horse is patient the colt soon learns to stand — unless it happens to be a highly nervous, fretful colt.

After the colt has been driven a few times in this manner he is ready to be hitched to some vehicle. These training periods should not last too long, especially at first with a young horse — probably an hour or so is long enough — as they tire quite easily, and are apt to become stubborn or sulky if overdone.

The first time they are hitched to some vehicle and asked to pull and carry the neck yoke I like to use a sled type, such as the front runners of a bob sled, even on bare ground. A sled is quiet and the pull is steady. A few drives on this and they can be hitched to a wheeled vehicle that has more chuckle to it, and that puts pressure on the breeching on down grades. If they are of good temperament they soon become accustomed to different vehicles and situations, and learn to depend on the judgement of the driver. It is very important that a colt develop confidence in this manner.

Problems and Preventions

A lot of colts don't cooperate too well in the first few hitches. When one is pretty nervous about the whole ordeal after some preliminary training I use a "W" on their front feet for a few hitches. With this they can be easily controlled after they have learned that the "W" will render them pretty helpless if they don't cooperate with the driver. Most often after they have been dumped a few times a little tension on the "W" will make them see matters your way. If they have an inclination to try to run when something excites them the "W" easily changes that notion, generally with just a little tension on the "W".

A "W" can be made from harness parts, such as a back pad with three heavy rings spaced across the belly band and heavy bracelets with rings to fit snugly on the front ankles, and thirty feet of good, tough rope. Or it can be purchased complete from a harness maker.

I have used the "W" on colts that were barn balky, by taking the colt single and driving it away from the barn. When it decides to return to the barn you throw it with the "W". I often get up and stand on their ribs or sit on them. They generally get up thinking you are bigger and tougher than they are and are quite willing to see things more your way.

The "W" should be used with caution. Never use it on concrete or frozen ground as the teeth or knees of the colt can be injured.

It is natural for the colt to resist the "W", but you must keep his front feet tucked up until he accepts it and lays down.

It is good to take a colt down and render him hekpless for a short time. This makes him see that he is not so big and tough.When a colt is released from being put on the ground with the "W" he is thankful and grateful to the trainer, and seems not to remember that it was also the trainer who put him there.

Another aid to driving a colt is to have a "jerk line" on, which is an emergency factor. I use a fairly light, pliable rope. Run it through the outside hame ring down through the outside bit ring, then back around the hames on top of the collar and to the inside bit ring where it is tied off. This gives you a lot of leverage if needed and can be used without putting a lot of unneeded pressure on the broke horse. For this first training I like to use a large, straight bit known as a log bit. It is less severe on a young horse's tender mouth. After they are more accustomed to being driven their mouths toughen up, and one can determine what type of bit is best for your particular horse. Horses vary greatly — some are real sensitive or tender-mouthed while others have a tough, hard mouth.

Showing the jerk line or safety rope. With this you have a pull on both sides of the bit and can tuck their chin against the collar if necessary to hold a colt. It is also a good back-up in case of a broken line or line snap.

A front view of a colt with the "W".

Do's and Don't's

It is very important that a green colt is taught to hitch up quiet; that is, to have patience while being hitched. I generally do my breaking alone, and quite often break two colts together, so I have a snubbing post set in the hitch-up area, and tie the two colts to this post while they are being hitched. You should take your sweet time while hitching or unhitching, and be sure that everything is right. The colts soon understand there is no particular hurry about this matter, and will soon learn to stand patiently until asked to go.

A pair of colts waiting patiently to be hitched, tied securely to my helper, the hitch-up post

A pair of coming two-year old geldings tied together at both front and rear, and driving like a team should.

When hitching a colt, or a pair of colts, the lines should first be hooked to the bridles, then the neck yoke snapped up. I like the neck yoke carried fairly high on the colts so there is less danger of one striking a front foot over it in a temper tantrum. This done, it's time to hitch the tugs. These should be the right length so that the breeching is not too tight, but still not too much slack in the poll straps.

I generally tie the colts' heads together with their halters instead of with the bits. When driving two colts this sort of steers them and helps to steady them. If, after a few drives, one handles much better and furnishes the brains for the team, I change this and tie the dummy to the smarter horse's hame ring, using the lower (breast strap) ring. This gives the more advanced colt more freedom and helps to control the one that needs more guidance.

It is understood that these colts we are working with have been ground driven single and as a pair, and are pretty well used to the harness and to being controlled by the bit.

They will start off awkwardly when first hitched on a tongue, and might try to step over the neck yoke or try to turn around. It will take quite a bit of patience in steering them for a while in any certain direction the driver would like to go. This is where a broke, gentle hitch horses comes

Showing a jockey stick in use snapped to the lower hame ring on the left hand colt and to the halter ring on the other. This keeps an "in and out" colt in position.

27

in mighty handy, especially for the first few hitches. The hitch horse should be well-broke, quiet-natured and dependable as a silly old hitch horse can surely goof up a colt.

Colts should not be hurried too much for the first couple of hitches, and should be kept as quiet and controlled as possible. They get accustomed to a vehicle behind them quite rapidly if everything goes well.

I like to use the front half of a bob-sled for the first couple of hitches, then go to a rubber-tired wagon or cart for a few lessons with longer drives where there is more to see and some up-and-down grades.

They should be driven on a snug rein. This way they soon learn to depend on the driver for direction and you also have better control — more able to meet emergencies.

One needs a whip in hand, but it should be used lightly, and only when necessary to convince the colt it is you that are giving the orders.

Very often I find that a colt which is rather slow and cautious the first few hitches turns out to be a real good moving horse as soon as it gains more confidence in what it is doing. Don't expect to turn out a broke horse in a couple of hitches — it takes time and patience.

The driver should strive to remain calm in all situations as much as possible. A horse can sense it quickly if a driver panics or becomes tense. In other words, if the driver looses his cool the colt he is breaking is pretty apt to do the same.

The first couple of drives are very important to a colt as they are subject to a lot of strange situations in a short period of time. If all goes well I make these first hitches pretty short, especially with a young horse, as they tire quickly. But never unhitch a colt who is in a rebellious mood, as that is the way the next hitching will start out.

After a few hitches, if they are performing fairly well and being controlled pretty well on the bits, I give them a fairly long work-out and get them a little tired — and then urge them into a well-controlled trot. At first they may think, "here's a chance to really take off", but keep them on a tight rein and a slow trot until they are happy for a chance to slow to a walk again. A young horse tires quite easily so this shouldn't be overdone as their muscles are soft and in warm weather they soon sweat up.

After they have had several hitches and seem to be responding quite well I like to take longer drives, with more to see, so they learn to pass or meet strange objects with less fear, and also gain more confidence in the driver. Some are much worse than others about this matter of being frightened of strange objects and noises and it takes patience on the part of the driver.

After eight or ten hitches, if the colt is progressing pretty well, it is good to put him on something like a manure spreader with a quiet, broke horse, and do some actual work, being careful not to overload or discourage the colt in any way. With this they learn to pull and hold back and they become accustomed to noise behind them. Also they begin to get a feeling of being a necessary part of the place when they actually have helped with the work.

At this point I'm going to inject something that may sound a little far-fetched, or to some just plain silly, but it works or at least is a great help. I found through experience, it helps to sing or whistle to ease a colt's tension. No matter how bad it may sound, they tend to listen and other noises and distractions are lessened in effect. Especially on windy days, when they tend to be more edgy, this seems to help greatly to ease a colt. This also keeps them informed that you are right behind them and that they had better be good.

Never take any chances like leading colts through a gate when they are hitched to some vehicle. They can easily become frightened and you are in a dangerous place, with not much of a chance to control them.

Don't take any chances like leaving colts stand without being tied. They are kind of cautious about all this new treatment anyway and will take every opportunity to get away from it all. If they get half a chance to sneak away they will soon be going full speed ahead and you have a runaway horse — a hard habit to correct and a very destructive and dangerous event for man, beast, and equipment.

Don't be in a big hurry to get a green broke horse into traffic as motorcycles, trucks, trailers and vans of all kinds look pretty scary to them at first, and for good reason. It is best if they can meet traffic on the off side first. They usually soon adjust to traffic if they don't have too many bad scares during their first few adventures on the highway. When meeting traffic it helps a lot to talk gently to the colt as they get a lot of comfort and courage from knowing that you are right there with them, and that they are not facing this terrible looking, noisy monster along. Probably you are about as scared as the colt, but don't let him know it.

I have noticed that young horses that are put in crowds of people such as in parades are a little green or timid at first, but they see so much so fast that they soon pretty much ignore it all and pretty much try to comply with the driver. Of course it is understood that they should be pretty much cooperative before something like this is undertaken. Once used without mishap in a parade or some such occasion they seem to gain a lot of poise and confidence in both themselves and the driver, whose ulcers will quiet down, as he is overwhelmed with a feeling of having accomplished something he wasn't quite sure he could do.

Don't overload a horse. They are like humans if overtaxed beyond their strength. They soon tire, get sore aching muscles, and may develop harness sores and sore necks and shoulders. Good natured, willing horses can be balked and ruined by over-loading and by ill-fitting collars and harness. These matters should be well looked into and attended to.

Don't overtax a horse's wind or breathing. If doing heavy work they should be allowed to rest quite often, especially if the work is affecting their breathing. A horse that is driven or pulled beyond his normal capacity to work can become windbroken, limiting his usefulness and decreasing his value. In warm weather they should be watched carefully for signs of over-heating. They don't have a flashing red light, but excessive sweating and rapid, heavy breathing is a sure sign that the heat is getting to them.

In closing I will emphasize again that you should not trust a young horse too far until he has had a lot of experience and has proven to be trustworthy. Sometimes the most docile appearing colts can be the most impulsive and unpredictable, generally surprising you when it's the least expected. And again, a well-broken, trusted horse is a great asset when breaking colts.

Afterword

Merle Eldon Saxon died at his home on May 21, 1991, at the age of 82, after a year-long bout with cancer. During his last year, when he was largely confined to his chair, he wrote his life history. This history tells much about Merle, and even more about the lives of the people who preceeded him — and in a real sense, who preceeded all of us. We are honored that his wife, Rachel, has shared Merle's story with us and are pleased to share it with you.

Bob & Mary Mischka
Heart Prairie Press

The Life of Merle Saxon

GRANDFATHER DANIEL SAXON

My Grandfather, Daniel Saxon, one of ten brothers, was born in the Worchester area of Northern England. The family mainly worked in the woolen mills for which this area was famous. Daniel came to Pennsylvania to find a new life, as he was allergic to the atmosphere of the woolen mills. He first worked in the coal mines, then went west with the tide of humanity to Illinois, still working in the coal mines. In the late 1800s, after having a family of eight children and one stepdaughter, they migrated west to Sutton, Nebraska, where they rented a farm for a year. During that summer they filed on a homestead quarter-section of land at Morefield, Nebraska — a new and totally undeveloped area.

That fall my Father, George, and his younger brother, Charles, (ages 14 and 12), drove a team of horses from Sutton to the new homestead at Morefield. They broke the sod with a walking plow and built a sod house to which the family moved the next spring, *truly pioneers!*

Daniel and his wife lived out their lives in Morefield and are buried in the Morefield cemetery located on their homestead where the sod house once stood. Their children gradually drifted back to Eastern Iowa except for Jim (who never married and ended up in Albuquerque, New Mexico) and my Dad, George.

GEORGE SAXON

George (Dad) came to northeast Nebraska in the spring of 1900 after hearing reports of the bountiful rainfall from a friend who had lived in Morefield. Morefield was very dry, almost desolate in some seasons. Dad told of one season when the seed corn which was planted in the spring still lay in the ground, nice and bright, when fall came.

Dad arrived in Newcastle, Nebraska by train on St. Patrick's day, 1900. He always said the Irish were celebrating the occasion in a big way and everyone thought they were Irish. He worked at the Sencenbaugh Meat Market for four years, doing the buying of the stock throughout the area and butchering and processing. He was very good at this work. After four years he went to the Black Hills area of South Dakota, and worked at the government fish hatchery in Spearfish for two years. He then returned to Newcastle and bought a farm eight miles south of Newcastle, in the Silver Creek area.

Dad moved onto his farm in the spring of 1906. In June, 1906 he married Rosalie Price at the court house in Ponca, Nebraska. Rosalie had boarded at Daniel's place and taught at the Morefield school while George was still at home. She was from Crete, Nebraska and was a graduate of Doane College. Evidently this marriage was put on hold for the six years since George had left home. The neighbors said, "George went to town with a team and wagon one Saturday to do some shopping and he came home with a wife". She had come up on the train from Crete that day.

MY BOYHOOD AND WHITEFISH MONTANA

My earliest memories were of a farm seven miles west of Ponca, Nebraska — a valley with fresh water springs all up and down the valley. This farm home, like many others in the area, is now completely gone due the trends to larger farms and big machinery, as well as a tornado and a fire.

We left this valley home in the spring of 1914, as father had developed respiratory problems which he blamed on the dampness of the spring valley. We had a farm sale, which I well remember, though I was only 4 years old. An ugly man with a big mouth hollered over everything we had and someone took it away. How I hated to see him holler over the horses, which I truly loved.

After a few more days, and a farewell party, we were taken from our valley home to the train station in Ponca by Charley Crowfoot in his Maxwell touring car. This was my first ride in a horseless carriage. On down grades it would get up to 20 miles an hour. Charlie would look back at us kids in the back seat and say, "we're going lickity split".

We boarded the train and were on our way to a new life in a new world. The first five miles were quite exciting to me; the scenery gliding by and the clickity clack of the wheels on the rails. The next 1195 miles were tiresome and boring to a 4-y-old. Just imagine a family of six cooped up in two railroad seats for two days and two nights. I'm sure this included some wet pants. Poor mother!!

We arrived at our destination, Whitefish, Montana, in the middle of the night, in the middle of March. The fresh night air, high up in the rocky mountains, has quite a bite to it at this time of year. Waiting there for us was Dad's friend, Bill Beller, who took us to his farm home with a team and lumber wagon. I well remember that slow, rough ride to the Beller farm. I didn't think I would ever thaw out again. After a couple of weeks in this lumberjack's bunk house the folks decided that it was too rugged a life for little Nebraska-born kids. It stayed cold. I think we all had large tonsils. Dad rented a house in Kalispell and we moved in right quick.

The folks started a search for a suitable piece of land to buy and started buying equipment to operate a small farm. One of their first buys was a 2-seated top buggy which was our main mode of travel for the next ten years. Also a new majestic cook stove which served us well into the 1940's.

The folks decided, after much looking in this strange, new, unsettled country, on an eighty acre piece of ground. The railroad cut across one corner of the place. The small house and barn were a half mile from the LaSalle Railroad Depot and a country store and a mile from the LaSalle country school, where Everett and I attended school, and where we attended church and most social activities. Dad built a new home right soon and we had one of the nicest homes in the valley. It is still well kept and in use.

It didn't take much equipment to operate this place with the larger half in thick, green timber. It was fertile soil and produced bountiful crops. In the winter season Dad hauled cord wood to Kalispell which he had cut and cured during the summer. Everett and I often went with him as Dad liked our company. This wood was hauled by bob-sled, as there was lots of snow. The sled was pulled by a little pair of mules, Jack and Johnny. I used to get awfully cold on these trips but was always ready to go again.

We learned to experience sorrow on this untamed land. One hot Sunday afternoon Everett, Leon Yates, Pickhead Smith, and I were swimming in the Flathead river, not far from our home. I shudder yet at the dangerous feats we performed. Suddenly Leon Yates' father appeared on the bank and informed us that a good friend of ours, Glenn Cunningham, had just drowned a couple of miles from where we were. We got back into our clothes pretty quick. My folks took us to the funeral, my first. The Mother of the victim fainted. I sure thought it was a cruel old world.

We four boys and Dad sure liked living in Flathead Valley, and we thought that would be our permanent home. We loved to take trips with the mules, up into the mountains. We would pick huckleberrys and boy, were they good. Dad had a good business butchering cattle and hogs for town meat-markets and for neighbors in the area. He was sort of a Jack of All Trades. He also did carpenter work, and would shoe teams in the winter.

BACK TO PONCA, NEBRASKA

After nearly six years in the valley Mother decided she didn't like it there. She said she felt hemmed in by the mountains. So in September, 1920 we bid a sad farewell to our many good friends and neighbors, and to a country we loved. Dad travelled in an immigrant car with all his personal belongings, including Jack and Johnny and his dairy cattle.

Perhaps I have come down a little hard on Mother in the last paragraph. After all she was pretty much raised a city girl, and had been treated to some of the finer things of life; namely a college degree, music, and plays. There was none of this in this new, undeveloped territory — and she missed it.

We arrived in Ponca about September 20th, 1920, and unloaded our livestock at the stockyards — Jack, Johnny, one milk cow called "Old Jewell", and four or five part Jersey dairy heifers. We rented a house on the west end of Lower Street, next to the John McKinley farm, for the winter. Kept the mules and Old Jewell in the garage, with the rest of the cattle at the McKinleys. We kids were all enrolled in the Ponca Public School — Everett in fifth grade, myself in fourth, Buell in second, and Clifford in first.

Dad then rented the J. H. Millon farm, across the road from Dan Sullivans place. We moved there the first of March. We four kids drove a single horse, Old Bell, to school, a distance of about two and a half miles. That first year was quite a learning experience for us kids. Everett and I both learned to cultivate corn, and it wasn't easy. We also helped Dad at corn picking time, which was more tiring yet, but we thought we were big-time farmers. It was a very wet season and we lost some of the crop to flooding on this creek-bottom farm. So next spring Dad rented the Pat McCabe farm back up on higher ground. That put us further from school on a terribly hilly road, but we made it, mostly on foot. That was a good crop year but we lost our hog crop due to cholera which was very discouraging, as we had a fine bunch of pigs. Our dairy heifers which we had brought from Montana were now cows.

The next spring, 1923, Dad rented the Jim O'Conner farm, a much bigger place, and a lot closer to school. He had to buy a lot more equipment. We were full-fledged farmers now. Everett and I were fourteen and sixteen, and practically did a man's job all summer. We had an enormous crop that year but prices weren't too great. We loved this farm with good buildings and running water but old Jim decided to come back and farm it himself, so it was moving time again.

The folks decided to stay close to town, until we kids were through with school, so Dad rented the Hazel Stefien place in Germantown — just 35 acres. We sold off much of our livestock and equipment. Dad always said "It's no problem to move. Just put the fire out and call the dog."

Dad and Everett both worked on road repair for the County with teams of horses. I took care of cultivating the corn crop. We bought our first car, a new 1924 Model T Touring Car, starter and all. The cost of this wonderful machine was $425.

We stayed put for two years on the Stefien place, but the cash rent was so high and the brick house so cold in winter that we moved across the road to the Sam Bales property on March 1, 1926.

SILVER CREEK

Everett graduated from high school that spring. Dad started farming up on Silver Creek where he owned 80 acres of the original farm he had bought. He had built a granary and a horse barn, and he lived in the granary. He enjoyed batching and roughing it. That fall he bought an adjoining 80 acres from Darby McQuillen. This made a square quarter section farm, with meager but livable improvements. So in the spring of 1927 we moved to our own farm on Silver

Creek. We rented a house in town, near the schoolhouse, until school was out and I had graduated from high school. We all moved to the farm on Silver Creek as soon as the school year ended, and that was "Home Sweet Home" for years to come. No more moving every spring.

Dad, though not in good health due to asthma, worked hard, was a good provider, and was liked by all who knew him. Although he had turned 60 years of age when we moved back to Silver Creek, he was strong and worked continually except for Sunday when he would rest, read his Bible, and visit neighbors. When we moved back to Silver Creek Dad had a confidential talk with me where he said I was most apt to be a farmer of his four boys, and that he hoped I would stick with him on this new venture. Everett had already held jobs in grocery stores and lumber yards, so it was clear that he would not farm. I had a love for livestock, especially horses and cattle, which I had inherited from Dad. So we worked together, and enjoyed being together. We built up our livestock inventory, bought several new major pieces of equipment, and really enjoyed our country style of life — except that the economy was very bad. I'll just mention the fact that Herbert Hoover was president, which should pretty well explain the economy.

For four years after my high school graduation Dad and I worked together and worked in the two younger brothers whenever we could. There were good crop years but the economy remained very bad. I bought good young cow at farm sales, as low as $25 apiece, that would bring $700 at a sale today. Profits were small at these prices, but we liked our country style of life and the neighborhood in which we lived.

MY OWN PLACE

The spring of 1931 we decided to expand our operation. I was 21 that spring. You were considered a man at that age, and could vote. I and my next younger brother, Buell, rented the John Yusten farm, one mile south of the folk's place. Clifford, the youngest brother, was to help Dad on the home place. Buell had married in his senior year of high school, so it was convenient for both of us to operate this Yusten farm together. He furnished the housekeeper and entertainment, a little blonde baby girl. I mustered what credit I could to get enough horsepower and equipment together to operate this farm.

We enjoyed our summer though our "cash flow" was practically at standstill. Our pleasant housekeeper kept us well fed, mostly on what the garden produced. We had a milk cow, some laying hens and a garden — with very little but bare necessities needed from Louie Wellenstein's General Store in Martinsburg. Buell and I worked hard and had a beautiful crop until it forgot to rain. The oats crop was good but the corn was practically a complete failure. The overall farming adventure turned out pretty much as a disaster as far as financial gain was concerned. So I worked the roads between Ponca and Newcastle with mules and a fresno. Buell and his wife, Rachel, gathered what corn there was and then moved to Newcastle and worked in a garage. I batched it out on the farm. Thus ended our farm partnership which would have been a very happy and satisfactory experience if it had rained on the corn. We ended the season with empty pockets and a debt to our brother, Everett, who worked in the lumber yard.

I rented some land around the area for a few years as John Yusten moved back onto his farm and operated it — until I bought it from him in the spring of 1941. During the 1930's I bought, sold and broke horses and mules along with the farming, but the economy was not good, so the gain was mostly experience. Social life during this period was kind of controlled by the poor economy, but there were weekly country dances in the neighborhoods. Also each town had a dance pavilion, if you could afford to go. Saturday nights were big events in all the country town, especially Newcastle, which has always had an abundance of pretty girls. The theory that two could live as cheaply as one, but only half as long, always made sense to me so I planned to keep my contacts with the ladies strictly friendly and fun times. Sometimes it was hard to stay with this plan.

BUELL DIES

I must catch you up on brother Buell's life, as it concerns my story later on. He bought a truck and did local hauling, moving gravel for country roads — all hard work and pretty meager pay. Rachel had another daughter the spring of 1934. That fall he and his family loaded up the truck and headed for Northwest Montana where he hoped for employment and better pay. He could do most anything. He skinned logs from the mountainsides with a caterpillar tractor in season and worked on a dairy farm in the winter. Fate has a way of controlling one's life. In late December of 1935 he was stricken with appendicitis, and it ruptured. This was before penicillin. He battled peritonitis for thirty days but succumbed to it after it got into his lungs. On his death bed he sung, in his beautiful voice, "God will take care of me" and "Rock of Ages". This has been a comfort to his dear wife ever since.

Buell's family returned to Nebraska with the body, by train. What a brave but sad little group got off the train in Sioux City. One felt so helpless in trying to offer any words of encouragement to this broken-hearted little group. I helped what I could with the funeral arrangements, a new experience for me. Reverend Alva Hutchins had the funeral service in the Presbyterian church in Ponca during a mid-January blizzard.

Rachel moved in with her ageing Grandmother Mendenhall who was striving to keep the old Mendenhall homestead intact following the death of her husband, though she was in her 80s and a small, delicate person. This farm home was 10 miles from town and supplies. She also maintained a herd of milk cows which became part of Rachel's daily routine. I hauled a couple of loads of coal to them from Ponca that terrible, cold stormy winter, with team and sled, through fields most of the way. Otherwise I was afraid Grandma would have Rachel cutting wood to heat the house. Christmas was cold and drab for everyone that winter, and especially for this little family. But they always seemed cheerful and in control of the situation whenever anyone stopped by afoot or with team and sled, the only modes of travel.

The following growing season was just as hard to live with. Many days were well over 100° and it just about didn't rain. Then there was a hard winter at home with the folks. Feed was scarce and it was so terribly cold and stormy. Silver Creek road was closed to travel, except for horses, for six weeks.

Spring came slowly but surely in 1936. I traded a nice big pair of black horses in on a new International tractor, with a plow and cultivator — total cost $1212. We rented more land than the home place and put in a large acreage of corn for that period of time. The corn crop turned out a total failure. We stacked our oat fields, mostly Russian Thistle, for our livestock's winter roughage and bought cotton seed cakes for concentrate. They survived.

I worked for the government farm program quite a lot that summer, measuring cornfields for the agriculture program. Boy that was hot work, with many days over 100°. On July 4th I took Rachel and the girls to Crystal Lake and the temperature soared over 110°. This heat turned the corn white. I remember going home from the day at the lake, bushed and burned. The water was hot and the old Dodge didn't have air-conditioning. We enjoyed the day in spite of the heat. It was the fourth of July. Well, that was back in the "good old days", before we knew of all these modern conveniences.

Our burned up crops meant a long hard winter ahead, and it truly was, with week-long blizzards and extreme cold. How Rachel managed to keep the Mendenhall cow herd cared for is almost unbelievable, but she did. I pondered my situation that vicious winter. I never intended to go through life as a single man. I would be 28 that next spring. I had planned that the first time we had a good crop year, with fair prices, I would get serious as I had a couple of prospects in mind that were interesting to me and were responsive to any interest from me. When Rachel and her two girls had come home, I couldn't understand why, my interest in other women seemed to dim.

I talked with Rachel that winter about her plans for the future. She told me she was thinking of returning to Montana as she had good friends there and she liked the country.

I could rent the farm adjacent to the folk's place, the place where my folks started married life and where my brothers and I were born. Finances were bad after that terrible 1936 drouth and burn-out, but life had to go on. The old adage "where there is a will, there is a way" prevailed, and I rented the farm. Now I began to think seriously of my need for a helpmate and companion. It bothered me that Rachel was thinking of returning to Montana with those two little girls, which I dearly loved.

RACHEL AND I ARE MARRIED

When I talked to Rachel of my plans for the coming season she seemed quite interested in what concerned me. This encouraged me that she might be a little interested in me. I thought seriously about our situation. She was my beloved brother's wife, but he was gone from this life through death. I liked her very much as a sister. She had all the qualities I wanted in a wife, and more. I also liked her family background. Her father and I were good friends. So, armed with all these conclusions and thoughts, I walked the two and half miles one afternoon when it was fit to venture out (the roads were all impassable) — just to check on the fuel supply at the Mendenhall place. When I decided to leave after a fun time Rachel walked with me out to the snowbound road. We talked about the farm I had rented and my plans for the next summer. At this point I got a shot of bravery from somewhere and asked if she and the girls might consider being part of my plans. SHE FLEW INTO MY ARMS. That was the beginning of a love affair that has endured for over 53 years. I floated home that wintry afternoon on "cloud nine", with a great peace of mind.

To shorten a long story, Rachel and I were married as soon as the weather permitted. I got possession of the rented farm on March 1. On March 4, 1937 we rode on horseback to the Silver Creek Road. The old Dodge coupe could make it into Ponca from there, if you were lucky. We got our license and were married at the Methodist Parsonage with Rachel's sister, Virginia, and my brother, Clifford, as witnesses. A pretty simple service but the greatest event of my life. The little girls were happy to have "Uncle Merle" come to live with them. My parents were much pleased to keep Rachel in the family and Rachel's father welcomed me as a son-in-law — so we were off to a good start.

We put together a few shorthorn milk cows and a flock of chickens right away and were on the way to becoming full-fledged farmers. A pretty simple way of life compared to today, but we loved it, and have fond memories of our early years of family life.

It was quite a change for an old bachelor, who had lived with his parents most of his 28 years, but we enjoyed our life together from the start. I had a problem for sometime with some of my old drinking buddies, who hated to count me out, but with Rachel's prayers and understanding ways this was, in time, totally overcome.

Betty, a spindly little six year old, started to Powder Creek School that fall. Quite a walk, but she was game. Joanne, just three years old, liked her farm home and "Uncle Merle". We were off to a good start. We had a good crop that year and liked the company from which we rented, so our first year was pretty much a success. In the early winter our son, Robert Merle, was born. The girls were elated to have a baby brother and to the say the least, I was a proud father.

The next season the company that owned the farm moved the buildings south to the road, quite an improvement. We rented this place for four years and have fond memories of this period in our life. But compared to now, it was pretty crude living. We had a battery-powered radio which we enjoyed as a family. We watched, or rather listened to, Amos and Andy and The Great Gildersleeve. It was great entertainment at that time.

In early spring of 1939 our second son, James Dare, put in his appearance — a happy event for all of us. We now were a family of six and very content with our simple way of life and our growing family.

We farmed this place for four years, with pretty good crops and a growing herd of cows. We also developed some nice young horses which were our source of power. The Land Company from Omaha liked us and wanted to get us on one of their bigger and better places but the FHA farm loan program came out that summer. John Yusten wanted to sell his farm (the one Buell and I had rented in 1931), so we made a loan application. We got the first government farm loan in Dixon County and bought the Yusten farm.

Dear old Dad passed away in early May, 1940. His friendly advice and love for his family were greatly missed. He enjoyed his grandchildren, especially Betty, the oldest, as they would walk to the mailbox, a half mile away, and plan trips back to Montana in Betty's little blue car.

The spring of 1941 was a busy one. We moved to our own farm and were happy to be back there, on the John Yusten farm, as owners. In early September, 1941 (which I guess was a banner year for us), a darling little daughter was born, Janice Faye. She has always been a blessing to all of us.

We prospered in our new venture. We built up our cattle inventory and did well with our horse business. It was a mile and a half to school, but the kids never complained. It was also seven miles, over dirt roads, to high school in Ponca — but they all graduated. We sometimes now wonder how this was possible with the road conditions as they often were. There were no school busses, and no school lunches.

We had some problems, as most people do. Betty and Jim both had appendicitis. Jim had pneumonia several times. In the fall of 1943 our precious little two year old, Janice, was stricken with meningitis and was in the Sioux City hospital for six weeks. How grateful we were, and still are, for her miraculous recovery.

Rachel, a firm believer in salvation through God's son, Jesus Christ and in the power of prayer, vowed after Janice's recovery that she and the children would be in a house of worship every Sunday that it was possible to be there, and we were. I felt guilty if I didn't go. I was raised in a Christian home, but had wandered far from what I knew was right.

We enjoyed our way of life, and were a close family. Our cow herd had increased, and our horses were our pride and joy. We found a good market for our surplus livestock. The kids all pitched in at an early age and helped greatly with the chores and farm work. Rachel was excellent in the dairy department, as well as helping with the farm work. I couldn't have had it any better but, for some reason I couldn't explain, I would have restless times and end up with my drinking friends. This bothered me terrible because I didn't want my young family to know about this. Also my health was deteriorating from my over-active thyroid, which the medication was failing to control.

We did attend church regularly, thanks to Rachel's great love for the Lord. In 1947 a new work was started in Ponca, and Rachel thought this was the best place to take the children as salvation through Jesus was being emphatically preached from the pulpit. I'm sure, now, that she had me in mind also. This was a small group of people dedicated to the Lord — the "grass roots" of the Evangelical Free Church in Ponca.

The spring of 1947 found us operating on a pretty large scale for that period of time. We had purchased the folk's home place, and were now farming a half section of land. I was quite concerned about my health, but we had a good crop and paid off our farm loans well ahead of time.

I AM "BORN AGAIN"

In late spring, 1947, the "George Iowa Quartet" came to minister to the church members, in song and in testimony. They really drew a crowd. Our old church house was filled to over-flowing. With the Quartet was a young fellow, a brother to one of the singers. He gave his personal testimony and sang, "My Home Sweet Home". This was the first time I had heard this song and I couldn't get it out of my mind. His testimony also stayed with me continually. That night it was difficult to sleep and the song and testimony kept running through my mind. After chores the next morning I got on my tractor and went to the north farm to cultivate corn. I made a few rounds in the cornfield but that song, "My Home Sweet Home", rang in my ears as if I had a tractor radio. Finally I couldn't resist any longer. At the end of the field I turned the tractor around and shut it off. I got on my knees by a knotty old oak post and truly had a meeting with the Lord. I couldn't understand it. I cried like a baby, but was extremely happy. That old knotty oak was my shrine until we sold the farm.

I went home for dinner, as usual. I don't think I said a word about my experience but Rachel says now that she knew something had happened, as I was so happy and different. That night at a meeting in our church I made it known publicly that I had truly been "born again".

The year of 1947 was a banner year for us, both crop and price wise. The price of corn was $2.00 a bushel, something we had never seen before. Our newly founded church did well also, and had a nice group in attendance for a new work. There were five other churches in Ponca, and our group was not welcomed by these established churches.

I enjoyed my freedom from my unwanted habits but my thyroid condition was worsening very much. In February, 1948, Rachel and I took off for Rochester, Minnesota, to the Mayo Clinic, to get relief from my over-active thyroid condition. My great fear of this ordeal was greatly diminished after changing my way of life. Most of my thyroid was removed on February 22 at high noon, with several student doctors looking on. I had to talk during the operation so my vocal cords could be seen. It was a pretty rough ordeal, but the results were worth it. I had a blood clot near my heart a couple of days after the operation, and was given a 50-50 chance of survival. But the good Lord was at my side — He must have had work for me to do. This was quite a burden on Rachel and our young family, but they did a great job.

I gained strength fast and felt much relieved after the operation. With the help of Rachel and the family we farmed both places and had a good crop that season. The next year, early in March, I had my appendix removed. But with our family unity we again farmed as usual. The boys and Betty all learned to operate a tractor quite young, and were willing to do it, as was Rachel.

We had quite an inventory of Shorthorn cattle by now, and were probably milking 20 or so cows — selling milk instead of cream. This milk project financed our five kids through Ponca High School. We eventually worked our cattle herd into a purebred herd. Each year we sold excess milk cows and had a good bull business. I enjoyed dealing and meeting new people, and we made many new friends.

Horses were always our favorites. Like our cattle herd, we worked our horse inventory into an all registered herd, both Belgians and Quarter Horses. We kept stallions of both breeds.

Our little family was quickly growing up. Betty was teaching school and Joan worked at the Ponca Dry Cleaners. Robert and Jim both spent two years in the military, so our family life was changing fast. When Janice, our youngest, went to Lincoln to work for "Back to the Bible" our little world kind of fell in — just Rachel and me. It was a natural way of life. One has to accept the changes, and we wouldn't want it any other way, but we sure enjoyed it the way it was.

To compensate for the empty beds in our home Rachel and I spent more time in other activities — our church work and our livestock business. It was evident that there were to be no farmers in our descendants, so we sold the north farm, my folks old place. This gave us more time to promote our cattle and horses, which we enjoyed together. We showed horses at fairs and were in parades with our four-horse hitch of blonde Belgians — at celebrations in every town in the area. We enjoyed it very much. We didn't get rich at it, but we made a lot of friends.

We bought our present home and acreage, north of Ponca, in 1969. In 1970 we moved from our "happy home" in the Silver Creek Valley to our present home. This is our 20th year here. I am pretty much confined to my Lazy Boy chair now. Rachel is still spry and ambitious, and tends to my every need.

Merle Saxon